THE SECOND VOYAGE

THE SECOND VOYAGE

Eiléan Ní Chuilleanáin

WAKE FOREST UNIVERSITY PRESS

WAKE FOREST UNIVERSITY PRESS
WINSTON-SALEM, N. C. 27109

This book, published in association with
Gallery Press, is for sale only in the United States of America.

© Copyright Eiléan Ní Chuilleanáin, 1977, 1986, 1991.

The Second Voyage first published by Wake Forest Press
in 1977. Published in Ireland by Gallery Press in 1977,
revised and republished in 1986.

ISBN 0-916390-45-4
LC Card Number 90-072091

Cover and title page designed by Richard Murdoch.
Text designed by Peter Fallon. Text typeset by Redsetter Ltd. of Ireland.
Printed in the United States by Thomson-Shore

Cover illustration from a scene in Virgil's *Aeneid* by Master
of the Prayer Books (c. 1500), © Coke Estates Ltd., in library
of Holkham Hall. The assistance of Viscount Coke and the
Trustees of Holkham Estate is gratefully acknowledged.

Contents

THE SECOND VOYAGE

The Lady's Tower

Hollow my high tower leans
Back to the cliff; my thatch
Converses with spread sky,
Heronries. The grey wall
Slices downward and meets
A sliding flooded stream
Pebble-banked, small diving
Birds. Downstairs my cellars plumb.

Behind me shifting the oblique veins
Of the hill; my kitchen is damp,
Spiders shaded under brown vats.

I hear the stream change pace, glance from the stove
To see the punt is now floating freely
Bobs square-ended, the rope dead-level.

Opening the kitchen door
The quarry brambles miss my hair
Sprung so high their fruit wastes.

And up the tall stairs my bed is made
Even with a sycamore root
At my small square window.

All night I lie sheeted, my broom chases down treads
Delighted spirals of dust: the yellow duster glides
Over shelves, around knobs: bristle stroking flagstone
Dancing with the spiders around the kitchen in the dark
While cats climb the tower and the river fills
A spoonful of light on the cellar walls below.

Lucina Schynning in Silence of the Nicht

Moon shining in silence of the night
The heaven being all full of stars
I was reading my book in a ruin
By a sour candle, without roast meat or music
Strong drink or a shield from the air
Blowing in the crazed window, and I felt
Moonlight on my head, clear after three days' rain.

I washed in cold water; it was orange, channelled down bogs
Dipped between cresses.
The bats flew through my room where I slept safely.
Sheep stared at me when I woke.

Behind me the waves of darkness lay, the plague
Of mice, plague of beetles
Crawling out of the spines of books,
Plague shadowing pale faces with clay
The disease of the moon gone astray.

In the desert I relaxed, amazed
As the mosaic beasts on the chapel floor
When Cromwell had departed, and they saw
The sky growing through the hole in the roof.

Sheepdogs embraced me; the grasshopper
Returned with lark and bee.
I looked down between hedges of high thorn and saw
The hare, absorbed, sitting still
In the middle of the track; I heard
Again the chirp of the stream running.

The Absent Girl

The absent girl is
Conspicuous by her silence
Sitting at the courtroom window
Her cheek against the glass.

They pass her without a sound
And when they look for her face
Can only see the clock behind her skull;

Grey hair blinds her eyes
And night presses on the window-panes,

She can feel the glass cold
But with no time for pain
Searches for a memory lost with muscle and blood —
She misses her ligaments and the marrow of her bones.

The clock chatters; with no beating heart
Lung or breast how can she tell the time?
Her skin is shadowed
Where once the early sunlight blazed.

Site of Ambush

1. *Reflection*

You are not the sun or the moon
But the wolf that will swallow down both sun and moon.

They dance around but they must go down
You will devour them all.

The houses, flowers, the salt and ships
Streams that flow down mountains, flames that burn up trees.

You are the twining gulf Charybdis
Whose currents yield return to none.

2. *Narration*

At alarming bell daybreak, before
Scraping of cats or windows creaking over the street,
Eleven miles of road between them,
The enemy commanders synchronised their heartbeats:
Seven forty-five by the sun.
At ten the soldiers were climbing into lorries,
Asthmatic engines drawing breath in even shifts.
The others were fretting over guns
Counting up ammunition and money.
At eleven they lay in wait at the cross
With over an hour to go.
The pine trees looked up stiff;
At the angle of the road, polished stones
Forming a stile, a knowing path
Twisting away; the rough grass
Gripped the fragments of the wall.
A small deep stream glassily descended:

Ten minutes to the hour.
The clouds grew grey, the road grey as iron,
The hills dark, the trees deep,
The fields faded; like white mushrooms
Sheep remote under the wind.
The stream ticked and throbbed
Nearer; a boy carried a can to the well
Nearer on the dark road.
The driver saw the child's back,
Nearer; the birds shoaled off the branches in fright.

Deafly rusting in the stream
The lorry now is soft as a last night's dream.
The soldiers and the deaf child
Landed gently in the water
They were light between long weeds
Settled and lay quiet, nobody
To listen to them now.
They all looked the same face down there:
Water too thick and deep to see.
They were separated for good.
It was cold, their teeth shrilling.
They slept like falling hay in waves.
Shells candied their skin; the water
Lay heavy and they could not rise but coiled
By scythefuls limply in ranks.
A long winter stacks their bodies
And words above their stillness hang from hooks
In skeins, like dark nets drying,
Flapping against the stream.
A watch vibrates alone in the filtering light;
Flitters of hair wave at the sun.

3. *Standing man*
The last bed excavated, the long minute hand
Upright on the hour,
The years in pain scored up are scattered and their tower
Down: time at a stand.

And upright on horizons of storm the monumental crosses,
Lone shafts like the spade
Haunting the furrow's end, flourish when man's unmade
Wedged in stones, sunk in mosses —

Aching an upright femur can feel the tough roots close
Gently over bone, stick
Fast holding a smooth shaft. Only the flesh such strict
Embraces knows.

4. *Time and place*
The river still descends, finding
Dark weedy stones of a harbour,
Pale widowed houses.

Within, the slatted dark,
Glint of water on a ceiling
Shadow of balcony bars
Above the dark knitting
Across the shady presses
Where the dated jamjars gloom.

The jam hardens at edges,
The grey fur fastens:
Filth clinging at high tide.

Weakly the escaping tide
Alone remembering alone
Falling out of rockpools
Waiting for the once-for-all wind.

A weakened creature in a dirty cream coat
With bare legs and a cropped head,
An empty face, staggers away from the sea
And looks up at the sun with a waiting eye,
Alone remembering alone.
She fingers three coppers in her pocket;
The wind scratches her face —
Dryskinned, these skeleton days
No more aware than wind of the passage of sand,
Tolling of dead bells.
The wind heads for fresh water
Shaking dust on her sleeve;
Her parcel of bread grows mouldy,
The milk in her jug sours fast under the sun.
As she turns the corner of the square
Meeting a whirl of bicycle bells
The old man on the near bench
Has two new grey hairs.

Before the dead underwater shining,
Before the stream started
Sprinkling off the mountainside
There was the scheming and steaming of the original volcanoes
And the glaciers trailing south.
There were winds combing the rocks, loaded with seeds,
Repetitious layers of dust,
Leaves by the harvestful piling in corners,

Blankets of sun piled over
Heavy with light . . .
Forget?
   Then came the clay and the raven
At last the spade and winding sheet.
Now all their lives on the site of the ambush
They see the dead walking ignorant and strong
As on their dying day. The grey shoulders
Against a rainbow skyline approach again and stop
Approach again and stop. The child's neck medal
Grows glitters and breaks away spinning —
The ploughed field gleams against the sky
Furrowed over and harrowed
On the ancient graves —
        a clean sweep of clay
Leaves drifting up to the threshold of the sky . . .
Shuffled. Start again.

5. *March in a garden*
The windows, arched, the blue granite;
Branches of cherry reach
Abroad like bridges, host a songbird
That was an egg last year.

Low forsythia flashes
From shade of high groined trees:
A narrow path cuts the lawn
And left to right a dark male figure
Walks quickly, eyes dead ahead,
Leaves a straight wake
While on high the attic windows of the city
Peer like bulrushes over this broad calm pool of spring.

Elsewhere, in the garden where I saw them first
In nineteen-forty-nine, the shrubs bloom out of season,
Their roots in New Zealand, their names
Rusting on metal tags. The gardener
Is Michael Barry, who threw the bowl
And hit the Chetwynd Viaduct. He shakes hands
And asks am I married yet.

6. *Voyagers*
Turn west now, turn away to sleep
And you are simultaneous with
Maelduin setting sail again
From the island of the white cat
To the high penitential rock
Of a spiked Donegal hermit —
With Odysseus crouching again
Inside a fish-smelling sealskin
Or Anticlus suffocating
Back in the wooden horse's womb
As he hears his wife's voice calling.

Turn westward, your face grows darker
You look sad entering your dream
Whose long currents yield return to none.

7. *Now*
I am walking beside Sandymount strand,
Not on it; the tide is nearly at the new wall.
Four children are pushing back and forth
A huge reel that has held electric cable
They are knee deep in the water
I come closer and see they have rubber boots on.

The sand looks level but the water lies here and there
Searching out valleys an inch deep. They interlock
Reflecting a bright morning sky.
A man with a hat says to me 'Is it coming in or going out?'
He is not trying to start something, the weather is too fine
The hour early. 'Coming in I think' I say
I have been watching one patch getting smaller.

Other people are taking large dogs for walks.
Have they no work to go to? The old baths
Loom square like a mirage.
Light glances off water, wet sand and houses;
Just now I am passing Maurice Craig's
And there he is reading a book at his window.
It is a quarter past ten —
He looks as if he's been at it for hours.

8. *Site of ambush*
When the child comes back
Soaked from her drowning
Lay fast hold of her
And do not let her go

Your arms will be burnt
As she turns to flame
Yellow on your dress
A slight flowering tree

A muscular snake
Spidery crawling
Becoming a bird
Then an empty space

Seawaves overwhelm
Your arms your hair and
Wind bites them until
Shivering naked
The child exhausted
Comes back from her sleep

           — troubling for a minute the patient republic
Of the spider and the fly
On the edge of the aspic stream
Above the frail shadows of wreckage
The white water-plant glinting upward
While the tall tree adds a rim to its age
And water focusses to a fish jumping
The rims of time breaking slowly on the pebbles like a bell
Eyes slacken under the weight
As the saint's arm began to sag
His hand spread under the warm nesting wren
But did not give way.

The spider swayed on the end of his thread
A pendulum. The child came back from the well.
Symmetrical breasts of hills criss-crossed.
The trees grew over the sun.

Swineherd

When all this is over, said the swineherd,
I mean to retire, where
Nobody will have heard about my special skills
And conversation is mainly about the weather.

I intend to learn how to make coffee, at least as well
As the Portuguese lay-sister in the kitchen
And polish the brass fenders every day.
I want to lie awake at night
Listening to cream crawling to the top of the jug
And the water lying soft in the cistern.

I want to see an orchard where the trees grow in straight lines
And the yellow fox finds shelter between the navy-blue trunks,
Where it gets dark early in summer
And the apple-blossom is allowed to wither on the bough.

Barrack Street

Missing from the scene
The many flat surfaces,
Undersides of doors, of doormats
Blank backs of wardrobes
The walls of tunnels in walls
Made by the wires of bells, and the shadows of square spaces
Left high on kitchen walls
By the removal of those bells on their boards,

The returning minotaur pacing transparent
In the transparent maze cannot
Smell out his stall; the angles all move towards him,
No alcove to rest his horns.
At dawn he collapses in the garden where
The delicate wise slug is caressing
Ribbed undersides of blue cabbage leaves
While on top of them rain dances.

As the fog descends
What will I do in winter? he thinks
Shocked by the echoing blows
Of logs unloading in courtyards
Close by, on every side.

Atlantis

1.
Here I float in my glass bowl,
Light wavering in water:
A thread shivers binding me
To a branching of dry pine,
I kneel in my white nightdress
And the watchful fish slide past.

A cold place with the spring tide
Pulling out there like horses
But safe. Don't ever mention
Atlantis underwater;
The glass barriers are much
Stronger than waves or high rocks.

2.
The staggering gable . . .
The baby dies on the doorstep
The old mother on the hearthstone,
The globed eye expels
Serrated dust in tears.

Odysseus Meets the Ghosts of the Women

There also he saw
The celebrated women
And in death they looked askance;
He stood and faced them,
Shadows flocked by the dying ram
To sup the dark blood flowing at his heel
— His long sword fending them off,
Their whispering cold
Their transparent grey throats from the lifeblood.

He saw the daughters, wives
Mothers of heroes or upstanding kings
The longhaired goldbound women who had died
Of pestilence, famine, in slavery
And still queens but they did not know
His face, even Anticleia
His own mother. He asked her how she died
But she passed by his elbow, her eyes asleep.

The hunter still followed
Airy victims, and labour
Afflicted even here the cramped shoulders —
The habit of distress.

A hiss like thunder, all their voices
Broke on him; he fled
For the long ship, the evening sea
Persephone's poplars
And her dark willow trees.

The Second Voyage

Odysseus rested on his oar and saw
The ruffled foreheads of the waves
Crocodiling and mincing past: he rammed
The oar between their jaws and looked down
In the simmering sea where scribbles of weed defined
Uncertain depth, and the slim fishes progressed
In fatal formation, and thought

                              If there was a single
Streak of decency in these waves now, they'd be ridged
Pocked and dented with the battering they've had,
And we could name them as Adam named the beasts,
Saluting a new one with dismay, or a notorious one
With admiration; they'd notice us passing
And rejoice at our shipwreck, but these
Have less character than sheep and need more patience.

I know what I'll do he said;
I'll park my ship in the crook of a long pier
(And I'll take you with me he said to the oar)
I'll face the rising ground and walk away
From tidal waters, up riverbeds
Where herons parcel out the miles of stream,
Over gaps in the hills, through warm
Silent valleys, and when I meet a farmer
Bold enough to look me in the eye
With 'where are you off to with that long
Winnowing fan over your shoulder?'
There I will stand still
And I'll plant you for a gatepost or a hitching-post
And leave you as a tidemark. I can go back
And organise my house then.

                              But the profound
Unfenced valleys of the ocean still held him;

He had only the oar to make them keep their distance;
The sea was still frying under the ship's side.
He considered the water-lilies, and thought about fountains
Spraying as wide as willows in empty squares,
The sugarstick of water clattering into the kettle,
The flat lakes bisecting the rushes. He remembered spiders
    and frogs
Housekeeping at the roadside in brown trickles floored with mud,
Horsetroughs, the black canal, pale swans at dark:
His face grew damp with tears that tasted
Like his own sweat or the insults of the sea.

The Persians

The dawn breeze came transparent spiralling out of the cliff
And the Persian host
Looked along the small path and saw (though not all
Really died that day)
That each had come to the place of his own death.

A man to flog the sea! But this was worse. Below
Already in the pass
The losers were attentive, longhaired. Too far to come,
A wave going nowhere.

Behind them only the captains waving whips.
No turning on the mountain road and hard to breathe:
By now their lives were nothing
But flowing away from them, breath blood and sweat,
Feeling the need of two faces
Or a wall.
                If there had been a wall
They would have climbed and then forgotten it. They had passed
All the valleys of darkness and now
Could remember only the ridges of the sea
And slowly climbing waves of sleep.

The body had changed, become the centre of their world
And the world changed
So the body could not live inside it, took off
Deathward, a high tide
Crowding round them like the towers of Babel again.
Poor straying barbarians. By now the rocks
Against them were blinding;
And one Persian thought about the patch of hard earth
Seen through a slit
In a jail wall, dear as a kind marked hand,

While one recalled, but could not think
Where he had seen it, a moving circle —
Sky over a high narrow tower
As blank and remote as a child's eye.

Manuscript Found in a Bottle

After a week at sea
They wake, the boards are damp
Easily rocking, sloped away
From the sun. There sits our captain on the right
Beginning the study of navigation
With an astrolabe.

A dark wall sways above, hides the rising sun,
The height of noon.
Upstage, long flat shadows like a railway station
Where the others crouch stranded.
Out of their stripe of darkness their quick breath
Ruffles the sheer daylight, while
They hatch small bundles towards angular death
Backing the cool wall, and one, a girl, watches for fish
In empty sea, crooning to the salt wave:
    Water soaks in wood
    You can sleep safe as
    Bats in a tunnel
    Water will reach you
    You can curl up like
    Cats on a mealbag
    Your whiskers will soon
    Begin to feel cold

The polar stars have left our sky,
Here in the lap of the wind it is cold;
Not an island nor a rock to mar
The slippery face of water —
At evening a whine, high up, of branches;
Flats of rain stretch out
Diagonal between the grottoes and sidechapels of the air,
The grey sea tilts at wind;
. . . And now far below the yellow sand revolves,
Our corner is thick with a drift of brown beechleaves.

Ardnaturais

The steel edge of water shuts
My close horizon, shears off
Continents and the courses of ships.
An island in a saucer of air
Floats in the tight neck
Of the bay, sealing
An intimate coastline. No pounding historical waves,
No sandribbed invasions flung
At high tide on beaches
Or violent ebb sucking pebbles away.

Warm death for a jellyfish, lost
Ten legs in a crinoline; the furred bee
Slants down from the cliff field, straying
Over salted rocks. The water
Searches the branching algae and my hair
Spreads out like John the Baptist's in a dish.
Shouldering under, I feel fear
As I see them plain: the soft anemone,
Bladdered weed, the crouching spiked urchin, rooted
In one clutch of pebbles, their long strands
Shivering under the light.

Alone in the sea: a shallow breath held stiffly:
My shadow lies
Dark and hard like time
Across the rolling shining stones.

Survivors

Where the loose wheel swings at the stern
Of Noah's ark, I can see the man himself
Deathmask profile against a late sunrise
Bleeding profusely from a wound in his throat.

On deck the mouse wakes up, stretches,
Edges to shelter to watch the cat.
The other mouse has stopped trying to distract him.
She does not know the beasts of prey
Have all been brainwashed. Their ascetic pose
Should last the voyage.

No winds compel us eastward or
Westward propel seeds of plants
Or the smell of decomposing systems.
If the water drains we may see
Again our flooded springtime, scarred
With damp, leaves clinging together
Like the pages of a sunk book,
The graves of the dead washed clean.

The bloodstained shirt stiffens
Turns brown at the shoulder; the blood
Edges down the sleeve, soft with a fresh smell.

The animals think they are being taken somewhere.
Do they all want to survive? They allow me
To lock their kennels at sunset, feed them
Turnips, even the carnivores.
Their drink is juice of the flood.

Please go easy with the blood.
It's not as if we had that much to spare;

The human ration has been cut
To a gallon a head, and the heads have been cut
As a temporary measure to me and you.

The menagerie expects a future and you
Crouching on the deck against my knees
Let it drip on my wet skirt
Soak in with dust and rain
Lodged firmly until the blood of the saints
Rises vertically smelling of ink
From sawdust, flagstones, seacaves, to explain.
While the blood still seeps down
I drink it steadily myself
(I have to think of the passengers)
My teeth ploughing in your throat.

I feel now so old I can barely remember
How it was before I was conceived.
I recall a shining egg-shaped ocean
Foul as a deserted egg;
It weighed down on the sea bed
Like the fat arse of Leviathan
Pressing the lives out of lobsters, cracking the ribs of wrecks;
Nothing was able to move.
How peaceful it was, long ago!

Ferryboat

Once at sea, everything is changed:
Even on the ferry, where
There's hardly time to check all the passports
Between the dark shore and the light,
You can buy tax-free whiskey and cigars
(Being officially nowhere)
And in theory get married
Without a priest, three miles from the land.

In theory you may also drown
Though any other kind of death is more likely.
Taking part in a national disaster
You'd earn extra sympathy for your relations.

To recall this possibility the tables and chairs
Are chained down for fear of levitation
And a deaths-head in a lifejacket grins beside the bar
Teaching the adjustment of the slender tapes
That bind the buoyant soul to the sinking body,
In case you should find yourself gasping
In a flooded corridor or lost between cold waves.

Alive on sufferance, mortal before all,
Shipbuilders all believe in fate;
The moral of the ship is death.

Foreseeable Future

Not immediately, but
The day will arrive for my last communion
When I plan to swallow the universe like a raw egg.
After that there will be no more complaining.

Why did I wait so long?
You may well ask: the plan is such an old one,
Even as a baby I might have been sucking away:
I might have cut my teeth on it,
Nibbling off a bit every morning.
I was too modest and doubted my capacity
To consume it all singlehanded; I feared
Dying and leaving behind a half-chewed world.

So I was perfecting the stretch of my jaws,
Padding my teeth like the hammers of a grand piano
To save the works from shock;
Like the crocodile that ate the alarm-clock
I mean it to go on ticking.
This is going to be a successful swallow.
How could I have lived so long
If I had not known that day
Was bound to come in the end?

The Ropesellers

Behind the black dancers and the snakes
A soft corner of sunlight, shady counters
Where new ropes are sold.
Pale coiled tight in ranks, piled
Spirals longer than a day's walk
Tight as a spring.

The dancers are circling, the music goes round and round
And around the necks of their charmers the snakes
Glide warmly, their heads waving, their wideawake eyes —
I can't find fear among the beasts and strangers
But I know it in the man who sits and smokes
Between two cylinders of rope.

The black dancers in the sun sweat.
The snakes follow the music, the rope
Is binding them all with burdens past their strength
That weigh like childhood;
A woman ties the feet of six live hens together
A knot binding us to the first day
A child strained to move a great bundle
That lay for years in a doorway, dusty but secured
With a new yellow rope.

The ropes are searching backward even yet;
They twine with the earliest roots of trees
Coiling around rocks, and the sources of streams.

Old Roads

Missing from the map, the abandoned roads
Reach across the mountain, threading into
Clefts and valleys, shuffle between thick
Hedges of flowery thorn.
The grass flows into tracks of wheels,
Mowed evenly by the careful sheep;
Drenched, it guards the gaps of silence
Only trampled on the pattern day.

And if, an odd time, late
At night, a cart passes
Splashing in a burst stream, crunching bones,
The wavering candle hung by the shaft
Slaps light against a single gable
Catches a flat tombstone
Shaking a nervous beam in a white face.

Their arthritic fingers
Their stiffening grasp cannot
Hold long on the hillside —
Slowly the old roads lose their grip.

Acts and Monuments

In imitation of the weed
Which, out of soft enclosing mud
As from a hand that holds a lead
Leans after the escaping flood,

Or when warm summer stunts the flow
In tangled coils lies tired and fine,
Or in calm weather stands tiptoe
To peer above the waterline,

The rooted trees bend in the wind
Or twist and bow on every side;
The poplar stands up straight and slim;
But their blood cannot flower or fade

Like weeds that rot when rivers dry.
Their roots embrace the stony plain,
Their branches move as one, they try
To freeze the effects of wind and rain.

And like the waterline the sky
Lids and defines the element
Where no unformed capricious cry
Can sound without its monument.

Letter to Pearse Hutchinson

I saw the islands in a ring all round me
And the twilight sea travelling past
Uneasy still. Lightning over Mount Gabriel:
At such a distance no sound of thunder.
The mackerel just taken
Battered the floor, and at my elbow
The waves disputed with the engine.
Equally grey, the headlands
Crept round the rim of the sea.

Going anywhere fast is a trap:
This water music ransacked my mind
And started it growing again in a new perspective
And like the sea that burrows and soaks
In the swamps and crevices beneath
Made a circle out of good and ill.

So I accepted all the sufferings of the poor,
The old maid and the old whore
And the bull trying to remember
What it was made him courageous
As life goes to ground in one of its caves,
And I accepted the way love
Poured down a cul-de-sac
Is never seen again.

There was plenty of time while the sea-water
Nosed across the ruinous ocean floor
Inquiring for the ruinous door of the womb
And found the soul of Vercingetorix
Cramped in a jamjar
Who was starved to death in a dry cistern
In Rome in 46 B.C.

Do not expect to feel so free on land.

More Islands

A child afraid of islands, their dry
Moonlit shoulders, sees in a deep gutter
A stone, a knot in the stream.
She feels the gasping of wrecks,
Cormorants and lighthouses.

She grows up to detest airports
But feels the sea in the waves of her hair
And icebergs in a storm of lemonade.

She knows there are some islands the sea avoids.
Boats leaving the coastline are led far astray
By strong currents, long mackerel shoals.
High on their dark rocks a man
Shouting for help, a bell ringing
Can call over hundreds of high tides
And not be heard, raising no echo
Until an injured seagull blown flat along the stones
Touches the hard earth, or the first fire
Lit by a castaway cuts the darkness
Liberating silence.

Go on Sailing

i.m. Paddy MacNeice

Now you will never see
The holly-trees cut down
The houses falling
The arrival of the stellar birds
Or your children's children.

Dear astronaut,
Continue to explore
The chambers of the earth
Winding between the submerged shells;
Dear Argonaut,
Go on sailing
To the centre of the planet.

Lost Star

Starting from the window, the bars
And the three brick walls, the cherry tree
In the centre of the yard, most of its leaves
Lying light as feathers beneath, but some
Still clinging by twos and threes —
Not enough to shield the planet
Hanging there like a fruit

But further away than it seems —
Can I really see you swinging
Around me now in a circle
Whose radius is longer than the arms of any known clock?

The lonely pilot guides
The lost star, its passengers the crowd
Of innocents exiled in winter.
Sometimes, letting the vessel drift
Into danger, he pauses
To feed them at his miraculous breast.

Distant as the spirit imprisoned
In a bronze vase buried in shingle
At the clean edge of the sea,
Floating like instantaneous foam or an island,
Sealed off like a womb,

Here where I sit so still
I can see the milk in my glass is tidal
Inclining towards you across the dangerous sky.

House of the Dead

What wind agitates the dust
Inside the Etruscan tombs?
They made beds for man and wife; the servants
Were buried in the hallway.
They sealed the door up and left the dead alone.

The dust in your pockets lay still;
You stretched out for your glass,
Blind as an old man in a dead calm.

Now your face looks innocent
As the Atlantic stirred up in storm,
Rattling its plenty on the pebbles.
The wind roared through your house and swept it clean.

Ransom

The payment always has to be in kind;
Easy to forget, travelling in safety,
Until the demand comes in.

Do not think him unkind, but begin
To search for the stuff he will accept.
It is not made easy;
A salmon, marten-skin, a cow's horn,
A live cricket. Ants have helped me
To sort the millet and barley grains.
I have washed bloodstains from the enchanted shirt.

I left home early
Walking up the stony bed
Of a shallow river, meaning to collect
The breast-feathers of thousands of little birds
To thatch a house and barn.
It was a fine morning, the fields
Spreading out on each side
At the beginning of a story,
Steam rising off the river.
I was unarmed, the only bird
A lark singing out of reach:
I looked forward to my journey.

A Midwinter Prayer

In winter's early days, the exile takes the road —
Dangerous nights with ghosts abroad:
The eve of Samhain in the High King's hall
Fionn stood all night, his eyes open
For well-armed demons, for fire, music and death.

The wanderer catches light from chapel doors.

    (He recalls a little boy running
    Up and down the same steps
    Doing the Ins and Outs:
    A Plenary Indulgence every five minutes
    To lighten the penance of Fenian men
    Awaiting liberation from demons underground.)

In silence the festival begins,
Human words are all spilled and soaked into the brown earth.
The silent holiday of Munster
Where the dead lie more at ease
Warmer than ever under the loud northern
Remembrance. The uprooted love
That fed them once collapses
Into their graves like cut flowers.

The final Sunday after Pentecost the priest
Announced the Last Day, when the dead will spring
Like shrubs from quaking earth.
Against that spring the dark night sways
Swelling grey plumes of smoke over the edge of the world.

    (He sees, westward again, the islands
    Floating lightly as bunches of foam
    Alongside the neat schooner. There
    Yellow apples constantly in season

Bend high branches, and the exile
Is comforted in an orchard.)

The road stretches like the soul's posthumous journey.
The holly-trees were falling already
When he left; the delicate high houses were rotting
In rain.

(He could remember summer barricades
Defended on top by a row of nettles)

And all his life seemed like a funeral journey
And all his company a troop
Of anxious gravediggers.
— And is that the young son
I carried through the wet and dry months?
Said the mother.

The air turned cold
Icicles began to grow,
Frost enamelled windows
And branches bent under snow.
All that the cold touched, alive or dead,
Changed. A time of plenty:
Ships tied up at the quay
Unloading crates of raisins, mandarins.
Yellow apples for the feast.

Touched by cold, the girl gave birth in a ruin:
Frost made angels echo behind the sky;
The cold stars offered gifts of incense and hard gold.
The snow spared the growing seed
As the year swung round to a new birth.

The exile is a wise man with a star and stable;
He is an unpeopled poet staring at a broken wall.
He tours the excavations of east and west,
He sleeps in a cart by a river
Blocked by old barbed wire and dead dogs.

When February stirs the weeds
He'll start again moving to the west
Rounding the earth to recover his lost islands.
He shelters in the ruined house
Where in dead silence the plaster falls
From ceilings, hour by hour. Those islands —
Under his skull, under wave, underground?

He walks the streets as the celebrations begin.
Work accelerates: turkeys are crated,
Bottles shift on shelves. He is jostled by baskets.

Now trampling feet remind his ears of hammers
Of a hundred smiths constructing the new model of the world
Turning in time to music or the circulation of the blood
Where love will not be out of season or a man out of place.
The seed laid in the dead earth of December
May yet grow to a flowering tree above ground.
He will sail in a ring of welcoming islands —
Midwinter, he can only pray to live that long.

Going Back to Oxford

Something to lose; it came in the equipment
Alongside the suicide pill and the dark blue card:
'I am a Catholic, please send for a priest'
With a space below for the next of kin.

Something to lose; and going back to Oxford,
Though not for good this time, I lose it again
As the city advances like an old relation
It's no use insulting.
Notice how she repeats her effects,
The Victorian towers after the mediaeval slum,
As a yawn turns into a shiver and the air
Bites like a mould pulling me north
To the evacuated roads.
Here the eye shrinks from what it sees,
The toothmarks are showing where the sharp spires got me;
And I agree to being chewed because
All that time I was looking for a reliable experience
And here it is: I give in every time,
Repeat the original despair.
This is where I learned it.

Because pleasure is astonishing, but loss
Expected, never at a loss for words;
Tearducts built in at birth: something to lose:
The best kind of innocence, which is not to have been afraid,
Lost according to plan; and here I am, walking
Through old streets to a familiar bed.

The Apparition

The circular white sun
Leapt overhead and grew
Red as a rose, darkening slowly blue.
And the crowd wept, shivering,
Standing there in the cold.

The sharp-eyed girl miraculously
Cured by a beggar passed the word along.
Water, she said, and they found a spring
Where all before was dry.
They filled their jars with the water.

All will be forgiven, good and evil together.
You are all my children. Come back
In mist or snow, here it will be warm.
And forget the perishing cold,
The savage light of day.

Every Friday at noon the same;
The trains were full of people in the evenings
Going north with gallons of sour water.

Deaths and Engines

We came down above the houses
In a stiff curve, and
At the edge of Paris airport
Saw an empty tunnel
— The back half of a plane, black
On the snow, nobody near it,
Tubular, burnt-out and frozen.

When we faced again
The snow-white runways in the dark
No sound came over
The loudspeakers, except the sighs
Of the lonely pilot.

The cold of metal wings is contagious:
Soon you will need wings of your own,
Cornered in the angle where
Time and life like a knife and fork
Cross, and the lifeline in your palm
Breaks, and the curve of an aeroplane's track
Meets the straight skyline.

The images of relief:
Hospital pyjamas, screens round a bed
A man with a bloody face
Sitting up in bed, conversing cheerfully
Through cut lips:
These will fail you some time.

You will find yourself alone
Accelerating down a blind
Alley, too late to stop
And know how light your death is;

You will be scattered like wreckage,
The pieces every one a different shape
Will spin and lodge in the hearts
Of all who love you.

Antediluvian

At some time previous to the destruction of the villages,
We find references to a young man 'about eight feet tall'
Naked and smooth with a knife loose in his hand
For pruning the lazy branches
Trailed across his path.
He showed up at one time or another
In several villages, but walked through
Without stopping or saying a word.
The people reacted with admiration and surprise,
Running to their doors to see, watching him out of sight.

And when the snakes were handsome in the grass
The people in the villages used to
Fill tin baths with enormous bunches
Of bananas, and carry them laboriously down
To the main road, and offer them to travellers.

Celibates

When the farmers burned the furze away
Where they had heedlessly lived till then
The hermits all made for the sea-shore,
Chose each a far safe hole beneath rocks,
Now more alone than even before.

Nights darker than thickest hawthorn-shade;
The March wind blew in cold off the sea.
They never again saw a sunrise
But watched the long sands glitter westwards.
Their bells cracked, their singing grew harsher.

In August a bee, strayed overboard
Down the high cliff, hummed along the strand.
Three hermits saw him on that long coast.
One spring the high tides stifled them all.

The New Atlantis

The feast of St. John, Corpus Christi Sunday,
Houses breathing warmly out like stacks of hay,
Windows wide, the white and yellow Papal flags
Now drooped: one side of the street nods at the cool
Shadow opposite sloping towards the canal's
Green weed that reflects nothing. Turn a corner,
Nettles lap at a high hoarding, 'sites for sale',
Empty window-frames, corrugated iron
In the arches of doors, old green paint softly
Blistering on gates. Cross a lane: a kitchen
Bare, darkening with one shadow milk-bottle,
Then a bright basement — a bald man in his sleeves
Folding linen in a yellow room
                              . . . Whose lives
Bulge against me, as soft as plums in a bag
Sagging at summer. New Atlantis presses
Up from under that blunt horizon, angles
At windows like ivy, forces flags apart.

The House Remembered

The house persists, the permanent
Scaffolding while the stones move round.
Convolvulus winds the bannisters, sucks them down;
We found an icicle under the stairs
Tall as a church candle;
It refused to answer questions
But proved its point by freezing hard.

The house changes, the stones
Choking in dry lichen stupidly spreading
Abusing the doorposts, frost on the glass.
Nothing stays still, the house is still the same
But the breast over the sink turned into a tap
And coming through the door all fathers look the same.

The stairs and windows waver but the house stands up;
Peeling away the walls another set shows through.
I can't remember, it all happened too recently.
But somebody was born in every room.

Night Journeys

There are more changes each time I return

Two widows are living together in the attic
Among the encyclopedias
And gold vestments.
                            A fishmonger
Opens his shop at the angle of the stairs.

The scullery I see has been extended,
A wide cloister, thatched, with swallows
Nesting over windows, now hides the garden.

I wake in Rome, and my brother, aged fifteen, meets
me. My father has sent him with a naggin of coffee and
brandy, which I drink on the platform.

And wake again in an afternoon bed
Grey light sloping from windowledge
To straw-seated armchair. I get up,
Walk down a silent corridor
To the kitchen. Twilight and a long scrubbed table,
The tap drips in an enamel basin
Containing peeled potatoes. A door half-open and
I can hear somebody snoring.

Dreaming in the Ksar Es Souk Motel

1.
The hard sand
Moulded like the sea
Sleeps out dawn
Planing east

In shallow scoops of light
Folding over caves and graves

She sails within glass walls
As in a ship, her mouth
Dry with air that hisses
In iron corridors

Her food smells of engines
Her share of water glows in a jug

A soft hum between
Her and the bird's cry
Outside she sees dogs
In dry riverbeds

Silent faces dark as the bark of trees
Pausing watch her drink

. . . There were roads
For wide-eyed fish muscling along
She could see palms waving mile by mile.
Here she never tasted salt, but backward
And forward in its short cage while she slept
The square swimming-pool pounded.

2.
Shift-click of night wave
Knight's move of current
Switching tides in a small square bay

To land below grey pointed houses looming
In clear air of daybreak
And a remote bell scares the flatfoot gulls
Walking up the ferry road
While from a chimney crest a blackbird looks
Severely down.

The bell rings seaward
Then reverberates uphill
Where the pale road curves away
Between dry white convent walls.

Standing on the wet flagstones you can see
Only the sidling road.
But follow the sound,
There are steps, lanes
High walls, darkness of sandstone
Valerian springing from cracks
Gutters and the ridges water makes in earth.

Out of sight the rivers persist
They riddle the city, they curve and collect
Making straight roads crooked, they flush
In ruined mills
And murdered distilleries.

3.
It has to creep like water, it cannot jump or spread like fire
It needs to labour past mountains to be lost
To see the drops fall in the still.
Like snow like sleep it grows
Like a dream it accumulates like a dream flows
Underground and rises to be the same
It feels the drumming of the hare and it fears what's yet to come
Suffering the storm and hearing the slates crash in the yard.

4.
In summer dawn a mirror shines
Clear in the surprising light;
The shadows all reversed point towards the sea.

At the Back Door of the Union

At the back door of the Union
A sad crowd gathered under rain
In a winter twilight is washed
By primrose light streaming out
Beneath a little cross from the humble porch.
They stand in groups like sheep and lambs
Drawn to admire simply a new-laid star.

Gazing inside the door, their eyes
Focussed to find one body, are shocked
At seeing two, an old woman's and a boy's.
Foreshortened in their coffins like two infants,
They are shrouded in tissue-paper instead of straw.

Seamus Murphy, Died 2 October 1975

Walking in the graveyard, a maze
Of angels and families
The path coils like a shaving of wood
We stop to read the names.

In time they all come around
Again, the spearbearer, the spongebearer
Ladder and pillar
Scooped from shallow beds.

Carrying black clothes
Whiskey and ham for the wake
The city revolves
White peaks of churches clockwise lifting and falling.

The hill below the barracks
The sprouting sandstone walls go past
And as always you are facing the past
Finding below the old clockface

The long rambles of the spider
In the narrow bed of a saint
The names inscribed travelling
Into a winter of stone.

Darkening All the Strand

The light neglects her face
To warm the fruited stone
Walls rising against her
Across brown spiral waves
Of the wandering Boyne.

What retreat, convent, group
Of Gaelic-speaking vets
Or Home for Protestant
Incurables, behind
Those pointed windows, breathes?

Somebody walked, along
The sloped geranium
Path to the damp steps where
A painted gate is shut.
New ropes hold a dark boat.

(Bright streak, brown shape.) Water-
Sodden, the near flat shore
Accumulates floated
Light weathered filterings
That shift under her feet,

The firm ground flood-riddled;
This historical shore
Clings to the evening shade —
A difficult stance for
Viewing the greenhouses

(Though sunlit to the left
Between a half-grown hedge
Plainly visible is
The nuns' graveyard, the small
Ranged uniform crosses.)

The cloistered Boyne gropes on
Washing out of the land's
Interrelated roots,
Under foundations, far
Streams the nuns may recall.

Cypher

My black cat lies still,
Washed, in the third of her lives
Veteran squatter, porte-malheur, she survives
Absorbing light on the sill.

While I wipe and scour,
Polish the glasses grimly,
The yard-shadow of the high crooked chimney
Slips closer by the hour.

What man forgets, at home
In the long noons of peace
His own imprisonment or the day of his release?
Could I forget this room

This view, the cleaning habit
All shared with Pussy?
Forsan et haec olim meminisse
Iuvabit.

Early Recollections

If I produce paralysis in verse
Where anger would be more suitable,
Could it be because my education
Left out the sight of death?
They never waked my aunt Nora in the front parlour;
Our cats hunted mice but never
Showed us what they killed.
I was born in the war but never noticed.
My aunt Nora is still in the best of health
And her best china has not been changed or broken.
Dust has not settled on it; I noticed it first
The same year that I saw
How the colours of stones change as water
Dries off them after rain.
I know how things begin to happen
But never expect an end.

Dearest,
            if I can never write 'goodbye'
On the torn final sheet, do not
Investigate my adult life but try
Where I started. My
Childhood gave me hope
And no warnings.
I discovered the habits of moss
That secretly freezes the stone,
Rust softly biting the hinges
To keep the door always open.
I became aware of truth
Like the tide helplessly rising and falling in one place.

The Prisoner Thinks about the Stars

The outsides of stars
Are crusted, their light fretted
With dead bodies of moths.

And moving the sound they make
Sibilant stiff moth wings
Drowns the universal tuning-fork.

They sing like whales over the prisons,
They almost bump the roof.

Wash

Wash man out of the earth; shear off
The human shell.
Twenty feet down there's close cold earth
So clean.

Wash the man out of the woman:
The strange sweat from her skin, the ashes from her hair.
Stretch her to dry in the sun
The blue marks on her breast will fade.

Woman and world not yet
Clean as the cat
Leaping to the windowsill with a fish in her teeth;
Her flat curious eyes reflect the squalid room,
She begins to wash the water from the fish.

A Gentleman's Bedroom

Those long retreating shades,
A river of roofs inclining
In the valley side. Gables and stacks
And spires, with trees tucked between them:
All graveyard shapes
Viewed from his high windowpane.

A coffin-shaped looking-glass replies,
Soft light, polished, smooth as fur,
Blue of mown grass on a lawn,
With neckties crookedly doubled over it.

Opening the door, all walls point at once to the bed
Huge red silk in a quarter of the room
Knots drowning in deep mahogany
And uniform blue volumes shelved at hand.

And a desk calendar, a fountain-pen,
A weighty table-lighter in green marble,
A cigar-box, empty but dusted,
A framed young woman in a white dress
Indicate the future from the cold mantel.

The house sits silent,
The shiny linoleum
Would creak if you stepped on it.
Outside it is still raining
But the birds have begun to sing.